Winning Ways

for Early Childhood Professionals

Understanding Toddlers and Twos

Gigi Schweikert

Name: ______________________________

Date: ______________________________

Redleaf Press®
www.redleafpress.org
800-423-8309

Also in the Winning Ways series by Gigi Schweikert

Being a Professional
Partnering with Families
Becoming a Team Player
Understanding Infants
Understanding Preschoolers
Being a Supervisor
Supporting Positive Behavior
Responding to Behavior
Guiding Challenging Behavior

Published by Redleaf Press
10 Yorkton Court
St. Paul, MN 55117
www.redleafpress.org

First edition 2013
Cover design by Jim Handrigan
Cover photograph © Ocean Photography/Veer
Interior design by Erin Kirk New
Photograph on page 4 by Amal Ayoub
All other photographs by Steve Wewerka
Charts on pages 16–17 are adapted from the National Network for Child Care, www.nncc.org.
Printed in the United States of America

Library of Congress Cataloging-in-Publication Data
Schweikert, Gigi, 1962-
Winning ways for early childhood professionals. Understanding toddlers and twos / Gigi Schweikert.
p. cm.
ISBN 978-1-60554-136-5 (alk. paper)
1. Early childhood education—United States. 2. Toddlers—Development. I. Title.
II. Title: Understanding toddlers and two.
LB1139.25.S3936 2013
372.210973—dc23

2012031930

Printed on acid-free paper

U22-07

Contents

From the Desk of Gigi Schweikert

That's me doing what I love most, working with children.

Dear Winning Ways Reader
(and Toddler Teacher),

When I started my first job as a toddler teacher, I was fresh out of the elementary school classroom. And although my degree and teaching certification was nursery through eighth grade (they probably don't even have a certification like that anymore), working with elementary school children and toddlers was not the same. I know; I tried.

For the first few weeks, I simplified my elementary and preschool lesson plans and set out to be the best toddler teacher ever. I wasn't. I couldn't get those toddlers to stop pushing the chairs around, let alone get them to sit in the chairs. I lived in New York City at the time, so I hopped on the back of my boyfriend's motorcycle—don't tell my mom—and headed up to Bank Street College of Education to buy every book they had on toddlers. I still refer to those books sometimes. Who knew I would ever get a chance to write a book of my own?

What I learned from my own experience and that of others during my years as a toddler teacher is outlined in *Understanding Toddlers and Twos* in a way that is simple and easy to read. The concepts are complex, and there's no way around that, since toddlers and two-year-olds are so complex. I hope the information helps you better appreciate and celebrate these children. They can be amazing and challenging all at the same time. If you work with toddlers and you love it, you have that toddler passion. You know what I mean, don't you? It takes a teacher with great patience, energy, and creativity to love toddlers well.

After you finish reading *Understanding Toddlers and Twos*, please send me your own thoughts, ideas, and stories about working with toddlers and twos at www.gigischweikert.com. I'd love to hear them.

Children deserve our winning ways,

Introduction

What's the *Understanding Toddlers and Twos* Workbook All About?

Welcome to the Winning Ways book *Understanding Toddlers and Twos.* This book is one of three in the continuing series that includes *Understanding Infants, Understanding Toddlers and Twos,* and *Understanding Preschoolers.* You can read all three or work with the one that best equips you as an early childhood professional. The workbook is designed to help you

- Develop a better understanding of the growth and development of toddlers
- Improve your interactions with toddlers
- Create a more toddler-appropriate routine and program
- Assist toddlers in their development of self-help skills such as toileting, dressing, and eating

Who Are Toddlers?

For the purpose of this book, toddlers are considered children from twelve to thirty-six months of age, or one- and two-year-olds. As you have experienced or can imagine, a wide range of developmental ability exists in this age group. Some programs group toddlers according to age, with younger and older toddlers separated, and others adopt a multiage grouping, especially in family home care and education settings. In center-based programs, classroom rosters are often designated by many factors: ratios, size of rooms, availability of space in the next age group, and developmental needs of the children. There may be children in your toddler room who have just learned to walk or who need more challenges as they are approaching preschool age. Your role as a teacher is to help each toddler thrive, regardless of classroom placement.

Who Should Read and Use the *Understanding Toddlers and Twos* Workbook?

Understanding Toddlers and Twos is intended for anyone who works with or is thinking about working with toddlers and anyone who works with adults who work with toddlers:

Veteran Educators Those who never tire of being with toddlers, have been toddler teachers for life, and can honestly claim, "I love them all," even the ones about whom most of us give a little sigh of relief when they are absent.

New Teachers Those of you who have just started working with toddlers and often question, especially in the midst of the children constantly pushing the chairs around and toddling about with endless energy, "What am I doing here?"

Career Seekers Those who are considering becoming toddler teachers. The early childhood field needs trained, enthusiastic, active individuals to care for and educate toddlers.

College Students Adult students in early childhood programs in colleges and universities.

Trainers Early childhood professionals facilitating seminars and workshops.

Professors Academics teaching adult students in early childhood programs in colleges and universities.

Program Supervisors Directors and other administrators who want to better support and train the staff in their toddler programs.

Stressed-Out Teachers Those of you who are burning out or giving in and need some new ideas and encouragement for your toddler programs. Toddler teachers tend to burn out quickly.

Parents Parents of toddlers, who in today's complicated world need support and advice on guiding their children.

Using This Book

Understanding Toddlers and Twos is divided into seven topics that you can read in their entirety, or you can select a topic that helps with an issue for which you need guidance. Although reading the entire book will give you the greatest insight into understanding toddlers, each area stands alone as an educational or training tool. Here's what the book covers:

1. Toddlers and Twos Are Amazing
2. How Toddlers and Twos Learn
3. How Toddlers and Twos Communicate
4. Helping Toddlers and Twos with Separation
5. Helping Toddlers and Twos Settle and Sleep
6. Helping Toddlers and Twos with Toilet Learning
7. Guiding Toddlers' and Twos' Behavior

Is the *Understanding Toddlers and Twos* Workbook Intended for Group or Individual Use?

Either way works great! You can use *Understanding Toddlers and Twos* as a training tool with a group or on your own. Either way, read through the appropriate content and complete the exercises throughout and at the end. Jotting down your answers will give you the greatest benefit from the workbook. If you are in a training group, having a written answer to refer to may help you feel more comfortable sharing your thoughts during the meeting.

DESIGN

How Is the *Understanding Toddlers and Twos* Workbook Designed for Training?

The workbook is designed so participants will

- Experience active learning by participating in discussions, solving problems, applying new knowledge to their current work situation, and getting reenergized about working in the early childhood field
- Connect current knowledge with the new material and have opportunities to talk about and share common concerns and issues regarding team building
- Gain practical knowledge and tips to begin using in their programs immediately

How to Use *Understanding Toddlers and Twos* in Trainings

You can use this book for a variety of training needs and situations. Here are some examples:

- Group of teachers from a classroom
- Administrative team
- Lunch and learn
- Staff meeting
- In-service day
- Partnership of several programs
- Community outreach
- Recruiting tool
- Local conference

winning ways

SELF-ASSESSMENT

How Much Do You Understand about Toddlers?

Take the following self-assessment to see how much you understand about toddlers. With toddlers' on-the-go approach to life and seemingly independent spirit, it's easy for early childhood professionals to think you know them. As a veteran early childhood professional, when I created the self-assessment, I was reminded and amazed about toddler development and surprised to learn through research a few things I didn't know. As you read each of the statements below and circle the frequency that best describes your understanding of toddlers, try to focus on how this information can help you improve your interactions with them. Be honest with yourself. Just because you know something is good for toddlers doesn't mean you always do it. Understanding your current attitudes and actions toward toddlers is the starting point for improving your role as a toddler teacher and making sure your interactions are positive and intentional.

1 I think toddlers are capable of doing many things.

Always Usually Sometimes Never

2 I realize that toddlers learn best through play, and my role as a teacher is to support their play.

Always Usually Sometimes Never

3 I understand that the speech development of toddlers varies.

Always Usually Sometimes Never

4 I pay great attention to toddlers who are having difficulty separating, because I understand that their fears are real and often intense.

Always Usually Sometimes Never

5 I help toddlers nap when they are sleepy and do not expect them to wait until predetermined naptimes.

Always Usually Sometimes Never

6 I am patient and encouraging when toddlers show signs of toilet readiness.

Always Usually Sometimes Never

7 I understand that discipline is not about punishment but about guiding toddlers to make safe choices and act in socially acceptable ways.

Always Usually Sometimes Never

Seven Steps to Understanding Toddlers

Refer back to your completed self-assessment form as you explore the seven steps to understanding toddlers. Whether you are on your own, reading and working at your leisure, or training with a group, you'll gain practical information you can use in the classroom and techniques for developing better interactions and relationships with toddlers and twos. Let's get started.

1 Toddlers and Twos Are Amazing

I think toddlers are capable of doing many things.

- Always
- Usually
- Sometimes
- Never

Are Toddlers Really Terrible? Don't Believe it!

Of all the age groups in early childhood education, I think toddlers get the worst reputation and unnecessarily so. Are toddlers really terrible? Absolutely not, and I take great offense at that commonly held myth, having been a toddler teacher myself for many years. Toddlers are learning how to be independent, how to socialize, and how the world works. Toddlers and twos are amazing.

123 Things Toddlers Can Do

Babble
Bang
Be alone
Be friends
Burrow
Carry
Clap
Climb
Climb around
Climb in
Climb on top
Climb over
Climb through
Climb under
Climb up
Collect
Converse
Coo
Count
Crawl in
Crawl out
Crawl over
Crawl to
Create
Creep
Cuddle
Dam up
Dig
Discover
Draw
Drip

Drop
Dump
Eat
Engage in doll play
Examine
Experiment endlessly
Explore with each sense
Fall
Feel
Fill
Find
Follow directions
Gather
Grasp
Hang
Hear
Help
Help themselves to wash, eat, dress
Hide
Hold
Hug
Imitate adult behavior
Imitate familiar acts
Imitate sounds and simple actions
Inspect
Investigate by trial and error
Jump
Kick
Kiss
Knock away
Knock down
Knock over
Lead
Listen
Look
Look for
Make sounds
Match
Meander
Measure
Mix
Mouth
Nest
Operate simple machines
Order
Paint
Pile
Pinch
Play
Pour
Pull up
Put
Put in
Put together
Reach for
Reach out
React to others
Read symbols
Rearrange
Recognize people and things
Rock
Roll
See
Select
Separate
Set up
Shake
Sift
Sit up
Slide
Smear
Smell
Solicit
Sort
Splash
Squeeze
Stack
Swing
Take apart
Take out
Taste
Tear
Test others
Touch
Transfer from one hand to the other
Transform
Transport
Tumble
Turn
Use tools
Walk
Watch

That's a lot of things that toddlers can do. Can you do everything on the list? Doing some of those things is hard even for me at my age. Toddlers are amazing, aren't they?

Who Toddlers Are and Aren't

It's easy to think of toddlers simply as being in between infants and preschoolers—middle children, in a sense. But toddlers aren't old babies or immature three-year-olds, and when you look at them like that you deprive them of being who they are and deprive yourself of appreciating and enjoying who they are. If you think of them as older infants or younger preschoolers, you will set up a program that is in many ways not interesting or challenging or one that is too sophisticated and may frustrate them. Either way, adults can easily develop negative views of toddlers, seeing them as terrible instead of terrific. So what's a toddler teacher to do? Think of the toddler stage of development as one of great merit, having its own particular characteristics, strengths, and needs.

Here are some of the not-so-positive generalizations that many people make about toddlers and a toddler's response to those thoughts, if she could tell you. As you read through the statements, try to think about how you could take that seemingly negative attribute and convey it in a positive way.

A Toddler's Response to the Not-So-Positive Things People Say about Toddlers

Toddlers are often messy. A toddler's response: "I sometimes look like a mess, too, with sticky hands and a goopy face. I learn with all my senses, and being messy and getting messy is what I do."

Toddlers are stubborn. A toddler's response: "I want to do what I want to do when I want to do it. I'm exploring the world. I have things I want to do too. Don't you feel that way sometimes?"

Toddlers are unable to share. A toddler's response: "I have to learn to experience ownership before I can learn to share. Do you share everything? Would you let another adult drive your new car or wear your expensive jewelry?"

Toddlers are not good listeners. A toddler's response: "I can't always understand everything you are telling me to do. Sometimes you give me too many directions at once. Sometimes you are asking me to do something that is too hard for me. And sometimes I am just busy with my work."

Toddlers often get frustrated. A toddler's response: "I do get frustrated a lot. I can't always tell you what I want with my words, and figuring out how things work in this world is a difficult job. Think about how you feel when you can't get your computer to work."

Toddlers never stop moving. A toddler's response: "I do like to move, but I always wonder why adults like to sit so much. My body can do so many things, and I want to use it to run and jump and climb. Why did you stop moving?"

Toddlers throw tantrums, hit, and bite. A toddler's response: "How can I tell others what I want if I can't talk? 'Use your words,' you say, but hitting and biting seem to work better. I don't like tantrums, either, but once I get started, I can't seem to stop. I need you to help me learn how to have more self-control."

The Real Scoop on Toddlers

Messy means toddlers are exploring the world. "I have to touch, taste, and smell everything to really learn. Imagine trying to learn how to use the computer if no one ever let you touch the keys."

Stubborn means toddlers are determined. "You'll admire my tenacity when I'm older."

Unable to share means toddlers are learning autonomy. "Learning to have control over things and the world makes me feel independent."

Not a good listener means toddlers are passionate about life and learning. "I am often more interested in learning about the world than getting a task completed."

Gets frustrated means toddlers are learning to communicate. "Until I can talk, read, and write, I'll have to tell you things in the best way I can."

Never stops moving means toddlers are whole-body learners. "I am learning how to use my body, and I like to practice a lot."

Throws tantrums, hits, and bites means toddlers are learning social skills. "Seems to me the easiest way to get something is to take it. I'm just learning all the rules of life."

Adults get frustrated too. I've always wanted to lie down in the grocery store aisle and kick and scream. I just haven't done it yet. How about you?

Expectations for Toddlers

To work well with toddlers, you need to understand who they are. The way you interact with toddlers, how you set up their environment, and how you plan their routine and activities should all be based on appropriate expectations. Are you expecting too little of toddlers, or perhaps too much? As I stated earlier, toddlers aren't infants, but they're not preschoolers, either. Good-quality education and care are based on an understanding of their development and an appreciation of the natural behavior of toddlers.

The job of toddlers, and all children, is the job of development. Take a look at the toddler's job description below and see if you have further expectations to add.

The Toddler's Job Description

As a young child, I am trying to make sense of the world around me. I learn by exploring, experimenting, and testing the limits of my environment and the consequences of my actions. I want to be responsible, independent, and capable, but it will take lots of experimentation, trial and error, and practice to get me there. Here's what I will do to ensure my success in school and life (and drive you crazy):

- I will use my curiosity to explore and learn about the world around me.
- I will be a unique individual in interests, in temperament, in moods, in how I learn, and in the care I need.
- I will develop at my own pace and in a way that integrates my interests and enthusiasm.
- I will let others know my feelings, needs, and wants by expressing myself in the most appropriate way that I can at the time through words, expressions, and actions.

- I will become a social being while maintaining my uniqueness and individuality.
- I will grow and develop in an environment that is safe and healthy.
- I will test all the limits by using my actions to check the reactions of people and things.
- I will use my body to determine the properties of people, things, and space.
- I will explode with energy because I love using my body to move about.
- I will explode with frustration because I have little patience.
- I will be contrary by refusing, defying, and resisting others because I am learning that I can exert control.
- I will be cooperative as much as I can.
- I will be responsible when I can.
- I will act silly because being silly is fun.
- I will experience separation intensely at times, since I have real fears when the ones I love leave me.
- I will develop self-confidence as I do things on my own and adults reassure me and show me approval.
- I will give hugs and blow kisses to show my love.
- I will snuggle on laps or cling to legs to feel safe and comfortable.
- I will expect the unconditional acceptance and love of the adults who educate and care for me.
- I will expect adults to accept and appreciate the wonderful person I am.

Some Developmental Milestones of Toddlers

Although every child is different and toddlers develop at varying rates, here are some things you can expect from them. Since development during the second and third year happens so rapidly, I divided the milestones into approximate lists of what one-year-olds and two-year-olds can do. Knowing what they like to do and what their emerging skills are will help you build a routine and environment that supports their development. For example, if toddlers like to move, and they do, how and where can they move in your program?

Physical Development

One-year-olds	Two-year-olds
Walk without support (usually by fourteen months) Walk backward (usually by two years) Walk upstairs Feed themselves (expect a mess!) Drink from a cup with help (anticipate spills) Stack blocks Scribble	Move (they are generally more active than at any other point in their lives) Run, climb, and walk up and down stairs alone Dig Throw balls Kick balls Jump with two feet together Stand on tiptoes Take things apart and put them back together

Social and Emotional Development

One-year-olds	Two-year-olds
Want to do things independently Have temper tantrums Play by themselves or beside other children May play with other children Have difficulty sharing May be possessive May not remember rules View themselves as the center of the world Are becoming more self-aware Show increasing fears Have rapid mood shifts (their emotions are usually very intense, but thankfully short lived) Like routine	Play simple pretend games Assert themselves by saying no Sometimes do the opposite of what is asked Imitate the behavior of adults and others Become frustrated easily Refuse help

Language and Cognitive Development

One-year-olds	Two-year-olds
Are curious Point to objects they want Imitate animal sounds Name familiar people and objects Combine two words to form a basic sentence Use the pronouns *me* and *mine* Name body parts and familiar pictures Use objects for their intended purpose Have short attention spans	Follow simple directions Use three or more words in combination Express their feelings and wishes Use objects to represent other objects Have limited attention spans Can memorize short rhymes Join in simple songs Think about doing something before doing it Want to make choices

6 Ways a Toddler Teacher Can Encourage Development

As an early childhood professional working with toddlers, you get to witness an abundance of growth and development in a short amount of time. Here's what you can do to encourage toddlers' development:

1. Know about child development so you can recognize the skills toddlers have mastered.
2. Recognize and delight in their emerging skills.
3. Provide many opportunities for toddlers to use and practice their skills.
4. Offer encouragement.
5. Provide help to avoid frustration.
6. Know that toddlers rarely need to be taught skills or pushed to perform emerging skills.

winning ways

Neither infants nor preschoolers, toddlers are increasingly mobile, autonomous, social, verbal, thoughtful creatures with constant urges to test and experiment. They have little language yet, so they use behavior to communicate. They are living contradictions: the erratic do-it-myself desire competes with the passive and completely dependent you-do-it. They are prone to change their minds about what they want. These restless, mobile little people have a drive to take apart the existing order and rearrange it, by force if necessary, to suit their own whimsically logical view of the universe. They are often charming and engaging but at times determinedly defiant or out of control with frustration or anger. Toddlers are very exciting people to work with, but their stage of development brings with it many challenges and considerable frustration for both the child and the adult.

Are you ready for the challenge? In the next chapter, I address how toddlers and twos learn. You'll explore the importance of play and how to create environments that help toddlers and twos interact with the world around them.

OPTIMIZE YOUR KNOWLEDGE

1 In your own words, answer the question, **"Who is a toddler?"**

____

____

____

____

2 Why do people often describe this age as **difficult**? What are some of the behaviors of toddlers that are challenging?

____

____

____

____

3 List five **positive** attributes of toddlers.

1 ______________________________

2 ______________________________

3 ______________________________

4 ______________________________

5 ______________________________

2 How Toddlers and Twos Learn

2

I realize that toddlers learn best through play, and my role as a teacher is to support their play.

- Always
- Usually
- Sometimes
- Never

Toddlers and Learning

Most early childhood professionals agree, and research confirms, that toddlers learn through play, yet there is an increasing push from society and some parents to increase learning in young children, even toddlers. I think defining learning is necessary in order to have a more thoughtful discussion. Everyone, teachers and parents, wants the same thing for toddlers: ultimately, success in school and life. How do you help toddlers move toward that goal?

Supporting Toddlers' Play

If play is something children innately do to learn and construct meaning of their world, then isn't it just something that happens naturally? Yes, to a degree. Children are curious and excited about learning. The way you interact with them and how you develop their environment can foster a greater desire to learn or can begin to stifle children's desire to explore and experiment. How can you support toddlers' play in a way that leads to a sense of self-confidence and continued curiosity? Take a look at the following list. Are you supporting toddlers' deep desire to learn?

Make playing with the children a priority. There will always be things to clean and items to stock, but are you really spending time down on the floor interacting with toddlers?

5 Ways to Support Toddlers' Play

1. Be involved in the toddlers' play, allowing them to make choices and at times take the lead.
2. Recognize and appreciate each child's natural skills and talents. You will see these interests evolve, even in toddlers. Some love music and others puzzles. Encourage children to try many opportunities.
3. Anticipate conflict and help toddlers resolve it. Give them ample space, ample toys, and ample time.
4. Keep children safe, but allow them to take risks that lead to greater learning. You know that one more block will topple the tower, but let the child put it on anyway.
5. Stay involved in play to help scaffold a child's skills to a higher level of understanding and learning.

How Toddlers Learn Best

The most successful learning for toddlers involves the following:

Encouragement Feeling loved, confident, and capable as a result of experiences with others, as well as being in an environment that allows for creativity and mistakes, facilitates learning.

Hands-on experience Toddlers absorb information through active exploration and discovery using all five senses.

Sequential activities Learning built on previously attained skills, precise sequence, and timing reflects individual differences; earlier is not always better.

Trial and error Toddlers construct meaning through direct experiences.

Social interaction Being with adults and other children reinforces learning and helps toddlers build new competencies.

Role modeling The greatest learning comes from watching others.

Learning Happens All the Time

It's impossible to separate learning from the routine and experiences of everyday life. However, you can do things to help toddlers have natural, developmentally appropriate experiences that enhance learning. What do these look like?

6 Ways to Guide a Toddler's Learning

Toddler teachers should

1. Pose questions, even to the nonverbal child
2. Provide an environment for discovery by rotating toys and providing interesting stuff to explore
3. Provide a sense of security to build toddlers' confidence to take risks
4. Allow for messes; sensory play is messy play
5. Be curious yourself—show enthusiasm
6. Provide an environment rich in many experiences

10 Steps to a Toddler Environment That Encourages Exploration and Learning

1. Teachers are actively engaged with children at all times yet know when to allow toddlers to explore independently or just pause and contemplate the world.
2. Every moment, especially one-on-one times like diapering and dressing for outside, is used to ask questions, label things, encourage the use of senses, and discuss what is around.
3. Provide a great appreciation for and access to nature: fish to watch, birds to listen to, nonpoisonous plants, open windows for fresh air, and water and sand for play. Toddlers spend a lot of time outdoors, not just in strollers but moving around.
4. The space is safe yet messy with evidence of exploration and learning: sand from sand tables, milk spills from toddlers who pour their own drinks, toys on the floor as a result of dumping. Such a space is messy a lot of the time; however, you organize and clean as well.

5 There are new things to explore every day: new books, pictures, experiments.

6 The environment has different spaces to be in, different feels, smells, textures, light levels.

7 There are many different centers for experimenting and playing.

8 The space has large-motor areas available all the time, since toddlers learn with their whole bodies.

9 Many different kinds of music are played at various times of day. And there are times without music.

10 The space is safe to explore, with few nos and many opportunities to explore independently.

5 Must-Have Good Learning Places for Toddlers

1 **"I can move around" places** Organize the environment so it's safe and child-friendly. Try to limit the number of items and areas that are off-limits to toddlers or that cause you to continually tell the children no.

2 **"I can make choices" places** Set out items and activities that require minimal adult supervision so toddlers can explore the environment freely.

3 **"I can touch" places** Offer toddlers materials they can hold and manipulate. Have one for each child when possible. Children learn best and behave better when it's hands-on.

4 **"I am valued" places** Have conversations with each child, asking him what he thinks and how he feels. Honor everyone's work.

5 **"I can have fun" places** Show enthusiasm and excitement about what the toddlers are doing and learning. Allow for messy and active play.

Beyond the Conventional Learning Center

Creating More Centers in Your Toddler Environment

How can you improve your indoor learning environment by using the following ideas in your room?

Combine centers. Put books in a cozy area, housekeeping and dress-up in their own area, and a sensory table and art in the same area.

Duplicate centers. Set up two book areas in different parts of the room and two sensory tables, one large and the other with small tubs.

Transform centers. Change a small table to a sensory area with a vinyl tablecloth, playdough, and plastic knives.

Enlarge centers. Make the dress-up area larger than the other centers if the children are most interested in that center.

Enhance centers. Add toy farm animals to the block area; put paper and crayons in the housekeeping area.

Create hang centers. Tape contact paper, sticky side out, to the wall or floor and let children put on and pull off bits of paper or string.

Prepare pullout centers. Bring out a bin of empty clean food containers and craft sticks for filling and dumping; bring out scarves tied on shower curtain rings for easy holding.

Establish child-initiated centers. Create a safe center based on where children go on their own. If they crawl around your legs when you change diapers, make a center to crawl in under the changing table by taking off the cabinet doors.

Have lap centers. One of the very best places for toddlers is in your lap; teachers have to sit down to have a lap.

Collect prop boxes. Keep theme boxes or other containers handy so you can pull them out when needed.

Exploration and Discovery

Toddlers are intrigued by real-world stuff. What do they do with real-life stuff? They sort, put together, line up, drop, fill, stack, and more. Toddlers combine the items in ways you might not think of. The best way to use these materials, if they are safe (and *safe* means safe to explore with mouths), is to just give them to the toddlers and see what they do with them.

19 Real-Life Things Toddlers Like to Play With

Although toys can be engaging for toddlers, you will see that items they can dump and things that they can push and places where they can stuff are the activities that keep their attention. What real-life things can you give toddlers to play with? The items on the list below may look like junk to many adults, but gather some things from the list and watch toddlers have fun.

1. Canning jar rings
2. Cardboard paper towel and toilet paper tubes
3. Clothespins
4. Fabric pieces
5. Funnels
6. Ice cube trays
7. Juice can lids
8. Large washers
9. Metal cylinders
10. Mixing cups of different sizes
11. Pinecones
12. Plastic golf balls
13. Plastic hair curlers
14. Plastic tubing
15. Shower curtain rings
16. Velcro pieces
17. Wooden dowels
18. Wooden spools
19. Yogurt cups

For added discovery, introduce a variety of small containers. Here are some possible containers:

- Backpacks
- Baskets
- Bowls of all sizes
- Boxes
- Buckets
- Containers in all sizes with lids
- Cups
- Cylinders
- Handbags
- Mesh fabric bags
- Paper bags
- Pillowcases
- Reusable cloth grocery bags
- Small cafeteria trays
- Tennis ball cans
- Wallets

Note that the real-life items you give toddlers to play with should be safe. Consider things made of many resources, like wooden bowls, metal containers, or even cups made of dried orange rinds. The possibilities are exciting and diverse.

winning ways

"IS THIS THING SAFE?"

A Quick Safety Checklist for Toys and Materials

Commercial toys are usually tested for safety and made of nontoxic materials. Bringing real-life things into your program is educational and exciting for the toddlers, but you have to be extra careful about safety. Use this quick safety checklist before introducing anything new.

- ✔ Is the item clean?
- ✔ Is the item large enough to avoid choking?
- ✔ Is the item free of sharp edges?
- ✔ Is the item free of parts that could pinch fingers?
- ✔ Is the item free of splinters?
- ✔ Is the item free of loose parts that could come off and cause choking?
- ✔ Is the item nontoxic? In other words, if toddlers touch it or put it in their mouths, will they be safe?

Tired of the Same Old Toys?

10 Tips to Make Toys More Interesting

1 Rotate toys by storing some of them away for a month or two. The toddlers will think they are new when you pull them out again.

2 Combine two toys. Put blocks with cars. Put plastic dinosaurs in the sand table.

3 Combine toys that don't seem to go together. Put out craft sticks with the playdough. Add markers and paper to the dramatic play or pretend area.

4 Trade toys with other classes.

5 Have a toy drive. Ask parents to bring in used toys. Select what you can use and donate the rest.

6 Check at local garage sales for good finds. Clean the toys well before putting them out.

7 Give children real-life things to play with like ice cube trays, plastic shower curtain rings, or cardboard tubes.

8 Wrap all the toys in recycled wrapping paper. The toddlers will have fun unwrapping them.

9 Look for toys that are not made from colorful plastic. In today's world, all the toys look the same.

10 Make toys. You can make musical instruments out of recycled materials like oatmeal containers or plastic milk jugs.

Toddlers are learning a lot about the world around them. It's easy to think that they're demanding and stubborn, selfish, and out of control. And at times they are, but they're so much more. Toddlers are learning the rules of socialization, and while they're figuring out how to act in a socially acceptable way, they'll make mistakes and so will the adults who guide them. So how do you keep up with little people who can't verbally express themselves, are habitually repetitive, and never stop moving? As early childhood professionals, you'll need to understand how toddlers learn best, have lots of patience, and wear comfortable shoes to keep up! How toddlers and twos communicate is next.

OPTIMIZE YOUR KNOWLEDGE

1 List three ways that you can **enhance** a toddler's desire to learn.

1 ____________________

2 ____________________

3 ____________________

2 Select one of the ten ideas in the "Beyond the Conventional Learning Center: Creating More Centers in Your Toddler Environment" box presented earlier. Then create a new **learning center** for your toddler program. Describe what you would do, or actually make and place it in a toddler room, noting how the children respond.

____

____

____

____

3 Name three safe, real-life things toddlers could play with and three containers they could use that are not listed in this book. Make sure to use the **Quick Safety Checklist** to ensure the items are safe.

Real-Life Things	Containers
1 ______________	1 ______________
2 ______________	2 ______________
3 ______________	3 ______________

3 How Toddlers and Twos Communicate

3

I understand that the speech development of toddlers varies.

- Always
- Usually
- Sometimes
- Never

How Quickly Are Toddlers Learning New Words?

By around twelve months of age, toddlers are beginning to move—that's what makes them toddlers—and beginning to talk—that's what makes working with toddlers so much fun. Their ability to learn new words is fascinating. Test your toddler language knowledge in the quiz below.

1 By eighteen months, a child can learn a new word every ________.

- (A) Two hours
- (B) Day
- (C) Eight hours

2 The average number of words a child uses at two years is 272 and at three years, __________.

- (A) 544
- (B) 301
- (C) 896

3 A two-year-old can understand __________ words.

- (A) 500–1,000
- (B) 1,000–2,000
- (C) 250–500

4 In contrast to a child growing up in a quieter environment, the child of a "chatty" early childhood educator or mom____________.

- (A) Is overstimulated by the constant chatter
- (B) Uses twice as many words by age two
- (C) Does not talk as soon

(Answers: 1. a; 2. c; 3. b; 4. b)

Learning to Speak Is Different for Each Toddler

The quiz above shows the rate at which typically developing toddlers acquire new language, but as I've mentioned before, children develop language skills at their own rates. Some toddlers utter several words as young as eight months, and other toddlers may not start chatting until eighteen to twenty-four months. We all know people who as adults never stop talking and those who are a bit quieter. It's the same way with toddlers.

Why Is There a Difference in Rates of Toddlers' Language Learning?

Toddlers develop language skills at different rates based on

- Individuality
- Communication experiences prior to care
- Learning a second or third language simultaneously
- Having older sibling(s) close to their own age

What do learning a second language and having an older sibling have in common when it comes to language development? Toddlers learning two or three languages may grasp the languages more slowly, and children with older siblings close in age may not talk as quickly because their siblings often talk for them and get them what they want. Language develops as a result of a desire to communicate a want or need, and younger siblings often get much of the attention and care they want from their siblings. What's your birth order? Ask the person who raised you when you began using lots of words. Did birth order or a second language play a factor?

Delay or Difference?

Does learning two languages at the same time account for a delay in a toddler's language development or just a difference? Interestingly, from eighteen months to about three to four years, the vocabulary of a child learning one language compared to that of a child learning two is the same. Here's the difference. That number of vocabulary words is divided across the two languages. So the toddler is learning the same number of words, but half of the words are in one language and half are in the other. If you look exclusively at the number of words the toddler knows in one of the languages, say English, then the child may appear to have a delay. However, if you note the number of words from both languages, the toddler's vocabulary doubles. So is it a delay or just a difference? I say it's just different, since the toddler has as many words. What do you think?

Some Speech Developmental Milestones for Toddlers

Around 15 months	Around 18 Months	Around 2 Years
Continues to speak gibberish Puts vowel and consonant sounds together Inserts real words into gibberish	Says nouns like *ball* or *cup* Names special people Says action verbs like *go*	Combines words to form simple sentences like "Me go."

What Is Gibberish?

Gibberish is the speech toddlers talk that doesn't make sense to adults but that often uses the intonations, pauses, and give-and-take of a real conversation. In gibberish, toddlers express the essence of language without using real words. Sometimes a real word or two may be imbedded in the gibberish. Toddlers may talk gibberish to themselves as they play or to one another or to you. Have you ever experienced toddlers speaking gibberish? Doesn't it sounds like their own made-up language?

Toddler Talk

List some of the words you hear toddlers say.

__________ __________ __________ __________ __________

What two words do you hear toddlers putting together to form their first sentences?

__________ __________ __________ __________ __________ __________

Progressing Speech

As children move from infancy to toddlerhood, parents and early childhood professionals often wonder whether their speech is progressing appropriately. Sometimes it seems like you're the only adult who can understand their speech, or sometimes even you can't understand it. That can be frustrating for toddlers and you. As with any skill that children learn, they learn language at different rates. Some pick up language quickly, and others move more slowly. Regardless of their progress, the important thing for you to watch is that language development proceeds steadily over a period of months, whether fast or slowly.

When to Worry

Although toddlers do learn to speak at varying rates, when should you as an early childhood educator be concerned about toddlers' speech development? The American Academy of Pediatrics suggests consulting a pediatrician or having an evaluation by a speech therapist if at about two and a half years of age

- Toddlers' speech is very hard to understand
- Toddlers don't use two-word sentences
- Toddlers don't follow simple verbal instructions

The Toddler Who Spoke English in Israel

Many years ago, I was a toddler teacher at the United Nations Child Care Centre in New York City. One of the young children I cared for, Itai, had parents who were diplomats from Israel. Itai spent his first two years of life in the United States learning English at the center and Hebrew at home. At two and a half years, he spoke only a few words of English and Hebrew—not unusual for a child learning two languages at once. At that time, Itai and his family returned to Israel, where people spoke only Hebrew to him. His mother wrote me a letter several months later to say that much to her surprise, Itai was speaking two-word sentences in English, even though no one was speaking to him in English. When Itai was in New York at the center, he was learning and understanding many English words, but it wasn't until he was developmentally ready that Itai could verbally express all the English he had learned.

What Can You Learn from the Story?

- Toddlers are usually able to understand many more words than they can verbally express.
- Toddlers are learning more than we think.
- Toddlers will speak when they are developmentally ready and able.
- Toddlers benefit from rich language experiences.

Can you think of anything else you learned from the story?

The Bottom Line: Speech Development Varies

Because toddlers' development of speech varies, it is important not to compare one toddler's language development to other children's language development. If you suspect a toddler in your care may have a delay, observe the child more closely, speak to your supervisor, and approach the parents about your concerns. Suggest that the parents speak to their family physician or pediatrician. The doctor may evaluate the child and/or refer the toddler to professionals who specialize in speech and language evaluation.

A Toddler Teacher's Perspective

"It is hard for teachers of older children to understand how much I talk during the day," says Ashley, a toddler teacher. "With young toddlers, I'm always putting words to their actions and sounds, so it's like I am talking for two. I say things like, 'José, you really like that milk,' or 'Look at you reach for that ball, Simone!' As a toddler teacher, I'm constantly talking, singing, chanting, telling the toddlers what I am doing, and reflecting their feelings. And of course, I try to listen a lot too. I'm tired at the end of the day from all that talking."

11 Ways to Talk with Toddlers

Children learn language by being with parents and early childhood professionals who encourage their efforts to communicate and who look for opportunities to communicate with them. Children also learn language in environments where language is valued as an integral tool for expression and organizing the world. Here are some ways to encourage communication and language development with toddlers:

Listen and respond. Take conversational turns that encourage give-and-take. Talk *with* the child, not *at* the child; watch for times that the child initiates conversation, and then respond. Let the child control the interaction sometimes.

Model language. Toddlers need modeling, not correction. Use words along with or instead of gestures, and use names: "Maya, please come sit in the chair," instead of "Sit here." Use nouns instead of shortcut pronouns: "Katie, take the ball" instead of "Take this." Adjectives enrich conversations and directions. Say, "Justin, find the red duck" instead of "Go get it."

Share books with children. Looking at or reading books with toddlers connects sounds and words with pictures. Share books regularly, even with young toddlers, who will enjoy the interaction with you, the sounds and the pictures, as well as the story line.

Give names to things and experiences. When a toddler points or says a word, connect the experience to words. When the toddler smiles at the sight of lunch, say, "Aben likes lunch, don't you, Aben?" When a toddler is upset or happy, use language to label the emotions: "Avril, you are so happy when you find the ball."

Extend the child's language. When toddlers combine words, early childhood professionals can extend their sentences. When the child says, "Kitty there," respond, "Yes, Rohan, the kitty is right over there by the apple tree."

Play with sounds and words. Language is a marvelously expressive tool. Whispers, squeaks, chants, rhymes, songs, and other ways of playing with sounds encourage children to explore the range and the pure fun of language.

Comfort with language. Use words to help children identify their strong feelings and to make them feel better. "It makes Ella angry when Gao knocks over your tower." Language is a powerful tool that can affect feelings dramatically.

Create experiences that use language. Provide objects and experiences that give opportunities to talk about animals, people, familiar objects, and make-believe.

Encourage questions. Ask toddlers questions to clarify and seek more information. Even before they have large vocabularies, encouraging questions by responding to quizzical expressions, gestures, or simple words is important.

Support the give-and-take of conversation. Help children listen to each other and ask each other questions. Help them attend to other children who are attempting to communicate with them, and encourage them to ask each other questions.

Know when to be silent. Give children the silent space to experiment with language.

What About a Toddler's Language Mistakes?

Language development takes lots of practice, and with lots of practice comes lots of mistakes. Toddlers may mispronounce words, use incorrect words, use third-person pronouns instead of first-person pronouns, and create the past tense of all verbs by adding *-ed* at the end of the word. "Me goed to chool" chants a toddler excitedly. You know that the correct sentence is, "I went to school." Your responsibility as an early childhood professional is to encourage each toddler's communication efforts and show your approval of those efforts. Take pleasure in the child's efforts to communicate instead of correcting mistakes. Children will learn how to speak appropriately more readily by listening to you communicate appropriately than by your correcting them. So don't worry about little language mistakes that toddlers make. They seem smarter than we are at times. Why isn't the past tense of *go*, *goed*, instead of *went*? Toddlers are more logical than the English language. Soon enough, you will miss the way they used to pronounce your name or how they said *spaghetti*.

Toddlers develop language skills at different rates. Your role is to communicate enthusiastically with them in a way that encourages them to develop language, helps develop their self-confidence, and fosters a love of words and language. Chapter 4 deals with separation anxiety. Helping toddlers and twos make the transition from home to school and from families to teachers and caregivers is often a big step for these little ones. Assisting them and their families with compassion and care during separation times is critical to helping the children feel comfortable in your program.

The next part of the book focuses on the importance of routine in toddlers' lives, and there's lots of opportunity to communicate with toddlers as you move through the routine of the day. Why is routine so important to toddlers and twos? Read on.

OPTIMIZE YOUR KNOWLEDGE

1 List some of the reasons that toddlers develop language and speech at **different rates**.

____

____

____

____

2 Name two reasons why you might have **concern** about a toddler's language development.

1 ______________________________________

2 ______________________________________

3 Explain why it is so important for a toddler teacher to speak **correctly and frequently** with the toddlers in her care.

____

____

____

____

4

Helping Toddlers and Twos with Separation

4

I pay great attention to toddlers who are having difficulty separating, because I understand that their fears are real and often intense.

- Always
- Usually
- Sometimes
- Never

Separation Anxiety and Toddlers

Even though separation anxiety is common in early childhood programs, there is often nothing more unpleasant for a toddler, his family, and you than a young child who is having trouble separating from his family. The child may cry, throw himself on the floor, grab the leg of the parent, try to run out of the room as the parent leaves, and cry for many minutes after the parent has left. The child is emotionally distraught. The parent feels sad, guilty, and frustrated all at once. And you are often stuck in the middle, wondering if you should try to distract the toddler, pry the child off the mother's leg, or step back a bit and wait for the parent's request for help.

What Is Separation Anxiety?

Separation anxiety in toddlers is a very real emotional experience. It is based primarily on their lack of understanding that their family members will return. Given that toddlers have little concept of time, they may fear abandonment. Toddlers may really believe that their parents are not coming back, or they may simply not want to be away from their parents. Although most toddler teachers easily become comfortable with separation anxiety, you should not minimize children's emotional devastation or become complacent in your reaction to each episode. You should always respond to each episode of separation anxiety with patience, compassion, and creative ways to help toddlers become interested in other things such as toys and activities.

12 Quick Facts about Separation Anxiety in Toddlers

1. Separation anxiety is common in early childhood programs, even excellent programs.
2. Separation anxiety is usually grounded in toddlers' fear that their parents are leaving and not in a fear of the classroom itself.
3. Separation anxiety is usually not an indication that the toddler program is inappropriate or that the teachers are uncaring.
4. Separation anxiety is a normal developmental stage.
5. Some children never experience separation anxiety.
6. Separation anxiety typically emerges between eight and fourteen months.
7. Separation anxiety comes and goes throughout the toddler years.
8. Toddlers may have a real fear that their parents will not return.
9. It's unclear why some children have a hard time recovering from separation anxiety.
10. Toddlers typically outgrow extreme separation anxiety, usually between eighteen months and two and a half years.
11. Separation anxiety may recur or intensify for toddlers during times of stress, such as a new sibling, moving, travel, divorce, a new teacher, or transition to a new classroom.
12. The attitude of the family and the helpfulness of the early childhood professionals can help to reduce the frequency and intensity of separation anxiety for toddlers.

Separation Times Are Learning Times

Helping children and parents arrive and separate should be an important focus of your work with toddlers. Guiding toddlers to separate from their families is an important part of your routine and curriculum, and you should carefully plan and frequently evaluate this part of the day. Toddlers are also learning to form attachments with people beyond their families, and that's you. How children begin the day in the program may determine the quality of their day. The ease or difficulty of separation may also determine the quality of the parents' day.

Drop-Off Times Don't Have to Be Hectic

If your arrival or drop-off times are hectic, you may need to rethink your staffing plans so you can help children comfortably settle. Perhaps other staff members can supervise the children who have already arrived so you can focus on the incoming toddlers and families who need your attention. Consider staffing patterns that provide more teachers during this important transitional time.

Separation Anxiety May Come and Go

Separation anxiety recurs throughout toddlers' and parents' experiences, sometimes unexpectedly and for no apparent reason. Often nothing can be identified at home or at the program that would cause a recurrence of separation anxiety. The likely explanation is that the cognitive or intellectual capacities of toddlers are developing so quickly that their perception and understanding of even a regularly occurring familiar situation, such as going to child care or preschool, can seemingly change overnight. Toddlers understand more and know more. Separation takes on new meanings as they develop new understandings of it, and these can cause distress. Hey, this is true with adults as well. Think back to a new love relationship when you were a teenager or even now. As the relationship grows, you develop new perceptions, understandings, and hopes: "What did he mean by that look?" "Why didn't she text me right back?"

Helping Toddlers Say Good-Bye: 5 Steps to Make It Easier

1. **Realize that separation is a real fear.** The fear and pain that come from separating is real for both parents and children. It is often hard to understand why toddlers who have been coming to child care for some time and are apparently settled in suddenly get upset when separating. It's easy to think that they should just get over it or that they will be fine. And although in most cases they will eventually settle, for the time that they are upset, that pain is real. It may be tempting for you and the parents to deny the reality of the pain. Even when children know the teacher and the program and enjoy it, and at some level know that their parents will return at the end of the day, the act of parting can be painful. I still get that feeling when I leave my family to travel for work. I am familiar with traveling, and they are familiar with me traveling, but that initial act of leaving makes me a little fearful and sad, and it makes my family feel that way too.

2 **Acknowledge the toddlers' feelings.** Early childhood professionals should always help children through separation times by acknowledging their feelings, giving them words to name the feelings, and comforting them. One of the many things children learn from adults in the early years is what feelings are appropriate in different situations and how to recognize and acknowledge their feelings. Being fearful or sad is okay, and it's your responsibility to help toddlers express their feelings. You must validate their feelings, not ignore or deny them. Simply distracting toddlers to stop the distress is inappropriate unless you communicate your acceptance of their feelings first.

3 **Use your words.** You might acknowledge toddlers' feelings by saying, "I know you are sad that Mommy left. Mommy's working, and she will come back this afternoon. Let's go play with the watercolors." Saying, "You're okay. Let's go play with the truck," ignores children's unhappiness. If they are angry in response to their parents leaving, you might say, "I know you are angry and you want Mommy right now. It's hard to wait for her to come back. Let's go play with the dough. That may help you feel better."

4 **Create a good-bye routine.** Use rituals and special objects to help children with separation. A special ritual or routine for children who are settling in can be comforting. It gives them a feeling of control, a feeling that "I know what is going to happen now. When Daddy leaves, my teacher and I go over and feed the fish." If your separation ritual for all children is feeding the fish, those fish might get way too much food. Here are some more rituals to consider:

- Looking out the window
- Setting the table for breakfast
- Getting a drink of water
- Looking for a special toy
- Selecting a book to read
- Waving good-bye
- Exchanging photographs; the child gets one of the parent, and the parent one of the child (be sure to get them back at the end of the day so you can do this again next time)

What other good-bye routines do you use or have ideas for? Write them below:

- ____
- ____

5 **Give toddlers something to hold.** It is natural for children to miss their parents during the day. Children new to the program may feel comforted by having an accessible object that belongs to a parent, such as a scarf or photograph. For some children, this seems to serve as an indication that their parents will definitely come back. This is a good example of how the minds of young children can work differently from those of adults. We adults know that the parent will definitely come back because their children are there, whereas for toddlers it makes sense that Mom will return to get her scarf! Having a photo of the family that toddlers can tote around can also be reassuring.

winning ways

"Does She Want Her Child to Cry?"

My Story about a Toddler's Parent and Separation

When I was a toddler teacher, I sometimes felt like I was going in a million directions all at once, especially at drop-off. Children were coming in with their parents, and we were serving breakfast, and I always wished there were two of me and two of the other teachers. Ever feel that way? Well, most of the children settled down to eat or play pretty easily after they said good-bye to their parents. A few had a hard time but calmed down within five to ten minutes, but there was this one parent who used to drive me crazy—actually, there was more than one, but that's another story. Anyway, this particular mom had a toddler who easily adapted to the classroom as soon as the parent arrived. The child would run off to play or see what was for breakfast and really had no separation anxiety at all. For me, as a toddler teacher, I wished all the children were like that. But for this mom, it was a different story. She seemed annoyed by her child being so comfortable with us, and every day she went over to her child to make a big deal about leaving for work. It seemed to me that this parent wanted her child to get upset and cry. The mom told the child things like, "I'll be back late this afternoon after naptime, so don't get upset if I leave. It will be a long time before I come back." And she paused, seemingly waiting for her child to run to her and cry, "Don't go," but the child never did.

One afternoon when the mom came to pick up her child, I told her that her daughter told me at naptime that she missed her mom. The mom started to tear up a bit and then responded, "I'm not sure sometimes if she ever misses me or even really loves me, because she never cries when I leave her." "She does love you very much," I told the mom. "Really?" the mom asked as she started to cry. I explained that the strong, loving bond they had was probably why her child could leave her mom so easily. I never would have thought that was what the mom was thinking.

What about the Toddler Who Separates Easily and the Parent Who Doesn't?

You would think that a toddler who quickly leaves his parents to engage in fun and exciting opportunities in the classroom would make any parent proud, but be sensitive to the emotions surrounding that seemingly positive episode of separation. Sometimes separating at the beginning of the day can be painful and difficult for the parent but not for the child. Parents' feelings need to be acknowledged with respect and empathy. This may be challenging for you. You may perceive that a parent's behavior and feelings are making separation more difficult for the child and life more difficult for you. You may be right, but look at why a parent might do that. Some parents or other family members of toddlers who easily say good-bye are often upset themselves as they wonder, "Doesn't my child love me? Why is she not crying like the other children when I leave?" So how do you help parents separate more easily? Take a look at the next section.

6 Ways to Help Parents Say Good-Bye

1. **Encourage parents to plan a calm, leisurely drop-off.** Saying good-bye is easier for most toddlers if the parents avoid racing in and out. You may prefer to have parents come and go quickly, and that works well for children who have anticipatory anxiety, in which the thought of the parents leaving is more anxiety-producing than the actual separation. But more often than not, parents feel more comfortable, and so do toddlers, when children settle down for breakfast or play before the parent leaves. Accommodate those times when parents are running late and a quick drop-off is necessary.
2. **Help parents establish a good-bye routine.** Saying good-bye is also easier when parents do not express uncertainty or ambivalence by saying, perhaps several times, that they are going to leave, then not doing so, or by leaving and then reappearing. Encourage parents to give a hug, say good-bye, and leave. A wave out the window helps many toddlers.
3. **Assist parents in saying good-bye.** When children are distressed, parents may feel as though they should not leave until their children are happy. Sometimes the parents are reluctant to leave because they are uncertain about leaving their children in your care. Parents who have difficulty separating require sympathetic assistance from you. Some parents will need gentle but direct advice about leaving if they are having difficulty knowing when and how to depart. "Can I help?"

is a good start. Follow it with "I'll hold David, and we'll wave out the window as you leave" to help parents know it's time to go.

4 **Avoid letting parents sneak out.** Parents may be tempted to sneak out without saying good-bye to their children, thinking this will be best for the children or anticipating that they will cry when the adults leave. Parents may think that sneaking out will help toddlers avoid the pain that leaving causes them. While showing sympathy for parents' intentions and pain, you should help them understand that it is never best to leave without saying good-bye, for this diminishes children's feelings of trust and security and may in fact cause them to become even clingier.

5 **Connect with parents during drop-off.** Separation needs to be thought of as a family affair involving the feelings and well-being of both parents and children. The value of talking, even briefly, with parents when they drop off their children is important. A system of exchanging written information on a daily basis is valuable as it supplements face-to-face communication.

6 **Communicate with parents after a difficult drop-off.** Nothing is more difficult for me as a mom than leaving my children when they are crying or upset. I feel guilty, can't concentrate on work, and wonder if I am doing the right thing, even when I know the competency of the teachers and the program. Communicate to the parents by call or text to let them know that their toddlers have settled down and are having fun. If children are still crying a bit, let the parents know that too. Be honest but reassuring. If toddlers are still upset, tell the parents what their children are doing, and reassure them that this type of behavior is normal. The child will settle, or you will call them.

Also encourage parents to contact you during the day to find out how their children are doing. It's easy to think that parents who call in are controlling, mistrustful of you, or even annoying. Try to view their desire to know what is happening as a good thing. When they reach out to you, look at it as an opportunity to build a trusting relationship with you, not just an inconvenience. Parents, like their toddlers, are all different!

A Quick Note about Toddler Pickup

The funny thing about toddler separation is that the same child who just as adamantly refused to let his parent go in the morning may be the one who just as adamantly refuses to go with that same parent at the end of the day. By pickup time, teachers and parents are often tired, but the children? They had naps. So they may be very content with what they are doing, and although they are happy to see their parents, they may want to stay and enjoy all the fun and activity.

My Toddler Reunion Experience

Once when I arrived to pick up my toddler son, he said, "You go back to work now." That kind of response didn't make me feel so good as a parent, especially when I had envisioned a more dramatic reunion, set to music and in slow motion, in which my toddler would run to me and I'd toss him in the air and we'd walk out hand in hand. Oh, well!

"I Don't Want to Go Home!"

Pickup Time and Why Toddlers Act the Way They Act

At the end of the day, most parents want an enthusiastic welcome from their toddlers and a smooth and pleasant exit from the school. Most parents want to pick up their toddlers and head home. Unfortunately, for a variety of reasons listed here, toddlers don't always respond to their parents' arrival in a positive way. They may demonstrate one or several of the following behaviors:

Ignoring the parents Ignoring the parents or giving them only cursory greetings may actually be a sign that children have adjusted well, feel secure at the program, and knew all along that their parents would return. In other words, this behavior could just mean, "I'm glad to see you, but it's no big deal. I knew you'd come back, and so I'll just continue with what I was doing." This is not unlike the way older children respond to being reunited with their parents or the way adults respond to short-term separations from people they are close to.

Falling to pieces Falling to pieces may be a natural reaction to the return of the person a child is closest to. It takes a lot of internal strength and stamina for young children to cope in a group setting, and by the end of the day, their self-control is low. Seeing that most special person, the one they know will love them no matter how awful they act, may just serve as a cue to act the way they feel, and the way they feel is miserable. Again, this is not unlike the way we adults cope with difficult days. We maintain a professional demeanor with colleagues, but when we get home with the people we are closest to and feel the most comfortable with, we let it all hang out and act the way we feel. Parents need to be reminded that children consistently behave better with you than with them. Toddlers often save their worst behavior for their parents.

Acting out Acting out, behaving in unacceptable ways, breaking rules, and defying limits may be young children's way of testing an interesting situation. There are two people, you and the parent, who sometimes set limits and enforce rules. "So, who's in charge?" Unable to articulate the question with words, toddlers ask the question through behavior. In fact, unless this is talked through with parents and expectations are made clear, parents will be uncertain and may think that while their children are at the program, you are in charge. You may be thinking the parents are responsible when they are present, and you may be looking critically at them and wondering why they don't give their children some much-needed discipline.

Resisting going home Being resistant to going home may mean one of several things: children may be expressing a wish for their parents to just stay awhile in this place that is special, to just be there. Or the toddlers may not want to suddenly end an engrossing activity. Or they may be saying something like, "I didn't like it when you dropped me off here, so I'm not going to go easily tonight." Or, anticipating the hustle and bustle that may characterize their world between now and bedtime, they may even be voting with their feet to stay in this child-centered place!

Share these possible explanations with parents so they understand that their children do love them. Parents may be thinking, "Well, it's happened. My son likes you more than he likes me. He'd rather be here than at home." (You may be thinking the same thing.) Parents may be embarrassed, sad, or annoyed. Of course, it is not always possible to say what children's behavior means, but the *least* likely reason is that toddlers actually would prefer staying with you instead of being with their parents. Parents need to know this.

winning ways

Helping toddlers separate and reunite with their parents is an important part of your program. It's an opportunity to interact one-on-one with toddlers in a group setting and a chance to develop positive relationships with parents as you work together to help children feel comfortable going from home to school and then back again. It's kind of like not wanting to go to a party or event, but once you do, you don't want to leave. Next, I address why toddlers and twos need sleep.

OPTIMIZE YOUR KNOWLEDGE

1 Why is it important to take **separation anxiety** seriously?

2 Explain what you can do to help parents who are **having trouble leaving** their toddlers. Write a plan and include what you would say.

3 Observe a toddler program at **pickup time**. Record the different ways in which the toddlers respond to the return of their parents.

5

Helping Toddlers and Twos Settle and Sleep

5

I help toddlers nap when they are sleepy and do not expect them to wait until predetermined naptimes.

- Always
- Usually
- Sometimes
- Never

Who Needs Naptime More—Teachers or Toddlers?

As a toddler teacher, I often thought of naptime as something to look forward to after a busy morning. You might too. I always loved seeing all the children in my class comfortably resting while I got a chance to eat lunch, chat with my colleagues, and catch up on paperwork. Sound like your thoughts? Hey, I knew there would be fussy kids on an afternoon when nap got interrupted, but I didn't realize the importance of daytime sleep and how it has the potential to affect the emotional and cognitive development of toddlers—positively, if the toddlers get enough sleep, and negatively, if they don't. But it makes sense. Let's take a look at the research that underlies this thinking, the ways you can notice and respond to sleepy toddlers, and the steps you can help children learn to move comfortably from a state of wake to one of sleep. Naptime is more than rest for you and the children: it's a biological need.

The Importance of Naps

Naps for toddlers are more important than you might think. Research about napping suggests the following:

Research Napping for children is a necessary behavior determined by their individual physical, neurological, and hormonal development.

Application If toddlers are sleepy, they should sleep. As an early childhood professional, you should not guide children to stay awake until naptime. Sleeping is a biological need. Think about it: you wouldn't make children hold their urine for long if they had to go to the bathroom. The same goes for sleep.

Research Adequate nighttime sleep does not eliminate the need for daytime naps.

Application It's easy for toddler teachers and parents to think that toddlers will sleep better at night if they don't nap for long. But nighttime sleep and daytime sleep are unrelated for very young children.

Research Very young children take naps because sleep pressure builds rapidly in their brains. Their need for sleep accumulates quickly during waking hours, and their need to nap becomes a biological necessity.

Application Toddlers are actively engaging with their environment and learning and growing exponentially. As they take in the world around them, they need to shut down by napping before they can process more. Helping toddlers settle into restful naps is an important part of your curriculum.

Research Sufficient daytime naps may reduce the risk of mood-related problems later in life.

Application By providing toddlers with the opportunity to sleep when they are sleepy, you are helping them increase their chances of greater emotional competence now and as they age.

Research The ability of toddlers to stay awake for longer periods of time during the day is an indication that their brains are maturing.

Application When toddlers move from two naps to one, it's not a matter of your routine or your adult prerogative to enforce those routines. It's simply a sign that their brains are developing or maturing and their need for daytime sleep is decreasing.

Research Toddlers who miss even a single daily nap show more anxiety, demonstrate less joy and interest, and experience more difficulty solving problems.

Application Although parents may have less flexibility in establishing a routine to ensure naps, early childhood professionals need to create a program that highly values needed sleep for toddlers. You should offer morning naps, afternoon naps, and occasional unexpected naps in response to toddlers' biological needs. Although they will occasionally miss a nap at home or in an early childhood setting, what might the long-term effect of many missed naps be on children's physical, emotional, and cognitive development? Based on the research, lack of sleep, including naps, may have more detrimental effects than we ever anticipated.

Happy Napping

How much daytime sleep do toddlers need? Again, the amount of sleep they need varies with age, maturation of the brain, and their activities prior to sleep. Interestingly, high-energy mornings don't always lead to toddlers falling asleep more easily or to a more restful sleep. A calming period of transition helps most children fall asleep more easily, regardless of the morning's activity.

Even with toddlers of the same age, great variation exists in the amount of sleep they require and when they require it. Use this table as a guide.

Daytime Sleep or Naps for Toddlers

Age of Toddler	Number of Naps	Duration of Naps
12 months–18 months	1–2	1 hour in the morning and 1–3 in the afternoon
18 months–36 months	1	1–3 hours in the afternoon

The Nap Experiment

At the University of Colorado–Boulder, Dr. Monique LeBourgeois conducted a study to understand how losing sleep affects the way young children respond emotionally to their world. The results, published in 2012, show that toddlers respond less positively to exciting events and more negatively to frustrating events. LeBourgeois says, "This study shows insufficient sleep in the form of missing a nap taxes the way toddlers express different feelings, and, over time, may shape their developing emotional brains and put them at risk for lifelong, mood-related problems."

Here's a brief description of the experiment. LeBourgeois and her colleagues assessed the emotional expressions of healthy toddlers one hour after their normal naptime when they missed a ninety-minute nap. They also assesed them again on another day following their normal nap. They videotaped the toddlers' faces while they worked on toddler-level puzzles featuring pictures of animals. Each child was given a puzzle with all the correct pieces and a second puzzle with a piece that did not fit. Investigators found a 34 percent decrease in toddlers' positive emotional responses after they missed a nap. The study also showed a 31 percent increase in toddlers' negative emotional responses after missing a nap when they attempted to complete unsolvable puzzles. A little sleep goes a long way. The big question, as LeBourgeois muses, is "The non-adaptive emotional effects we saw in toddlers who missed a single nap make us wonder how young kids who consistently don't get enough sleep deal with their complicated social worlds." What do you think? Can missing a nap really make that much of a difference, and what about the long-term cumulative affects?

One Naptime for Toddlers or Two?

Ideally toddlers should sleep when they are sleepy. I know what you are thinking. Hey, I've been a toddler teacher too, and it's great when all the children sleep at the same time: it gives you and them a break. But that won't always happen. And it's your responsibility as an early childhood professional to be flexible to the needs of the toddlers, especially concerning sleep. If you consider toddlers to be children who can walk or at least toddle, then those children may be as young as twelve months old, or even younger! Young toddlers especially should nap when they are tired.

Some toddlers may need a morning and afternoon nap, and others may just occasionally need that extra morning nap. Don't you have days when you need a little more sleep? Toddlers are growing and learning at rapid rates, and sleeping is the only way their bodies can replenish. Like us, toddlers vary in their energy levels and paces. Some children need to crash in late morning, while others will not sleep for more than an hour in the afternoon. Your program's nap routine, staffing patterns, and use of space must take into account toddlers who don't fit the 1:00 to 3:00 naptime.

Morning Naps for Toddlers

Are you flexible enough to allow morning naps? Take a look at the assessment below and rate yourself and your program honestly.

SELF-ASSESSMENT

Do I Allow for Morning Toddler Naps?

1 I realize that sleep, like food, is a basic need for toddlers.

Always Usually Sometimes Never

2 I understand that depriving toddlers of needed sleep can **diminish** their ability to concentrate, focus, and interact with the environment and others.

Always Usually Sometimes Never

3 I know that keeping toddlers awake or eliminating morning naps does not help them sleep longer or better in the afternoon or at night.

Always Usually Sometimes Never

4 I observe throughout the day sleep readiness cues in toddlers, such as eye rubbing, clumsiness, and being easily frustrated or uninterested in play.

Always Usually Sometimes Never

5 I create a routine that meets the needs of the toddlers in my care, and it includes morning naps for some children.

Always Usually Sometimes Never

6 I establish a morning nap routine that is good for children but not necessarily convenient for adults.

Always Usually Sometimes Never

7 I place cots or mats in less active areas of the room for toddlers who I know usually need a morning nap.

Always Usually Sometimes Never

8 I guide sleepy toddlers to rest on a cot or mat for a morning nap.

Always Usually Sometimes Never

9 I am able to balance midmorning nappers and the activity of the other toddlers in my classroom.

Always Usually Sometimes Never

Review your responses and make some changes to your routine and schedule if necessary.

Knowing When Toddlers Are Tired

Sleep Readiness Cues

Rubbing eyes

Showing lack of interest in play

Clinging to an adult

Sucking a thumb

Putting head down (in a plate of spaghetti is not good!)

Getting clumsy

Slowing pace of activity

Becoming very easily frustrated

Becoming fussy for no apparent reason

Lying down

Not Set Up for Morning Naps?

Balancing the needs of the group of children you care for and the individual needs of each toddler with the resources of teacher power is hard to do well. But ask yourself, "Am I expecting the children to follow my routine, or am I setting up a routine that works well for them?" You might be concerned that if toddlers nap in the morning, they won't nap in the afternoon. That might be true, but *no* research indicates that children who are deprived of sleep will sleep better and longer later in the day. In fact, the opposite is true. Children who sleep when they are sleepy sleep well; being overtired can cause them to have a hard time falling asleep.

Set up a cot or mat for the few children who may need morning naps. They will sleep through the noise and conversation of the busy toddlers around them. You'll know when children don't need that morning nap anymore, because they won't sleep. Some toddlers may not need a morning nap but could benefit from lying down on a cot for a few minutes and just being quiet. Be responsive to the needs of the children and be flexible in meeting those needs.

Helping Toddlers Sleep and Rest

Moving into and out of sleep are times when most human beings are very vulnerable. Naptime is an important time to be relaxed and gentle with children and to treat them as individuals. It is also time for individualized schedules and patience; these give toddlers leeway in settling down and waking up as they gradually make the transition to a group nap schedule.

If sleep times are based on the needs and styles of each child and variations are expected from day to day, napping becomes a natural, even pleasant activity. This is much better than an arena for confrontation or the dreaded countdown to rub all the backs as you try to get all the toddlers to go to sleep quickly and stay asleep for hours. Some toddlers sleep easily and predictably, while others resist sleep and have difficulty making the transition from awake to asleep.

Gently into Sleep

When possible, put the toddlers down to sleep the way their families do at home, such as with a special blanket, patting, or sitting nearby. You probably have your own going-to-sleep rituals. Do you nap? If you do, where do you like to nap and when? If you don't nap, think about your nighttime sleep rituals, such as taking a shower, watching TV, listening to music, or reading a book. Most of us slowly move from awake to asleep in a comfortable, predictable ritual. Even missing a special pillow can keep many adults tossing and turning all night long. Sometimes toddlers who will not sleep will rest quietly on cots for a while with a few toys or a book as quiet entertainment.

10 Ways to Make Naptime More Enjoyable for Teacher and Toddlers

1 Have a consistent routine with naps at the same time each day, but adjust your schedule to meet the toddlers' nap needs. This may be for a day or a long-term change.

2 Have the toddlers help you put out their cots or mats and make their beds with their blankets and any special comfort items.

3 Realize that even though you could put out the mats and blankets more quickly by yourself, involving the toddlers helps establish a better sleep routine.

4 Have a quite time after lunch and before nap begins so toddlers can slowly calm down.

5 Allow children who take longer to fall asleep to have a book on their mat for a while.

6 Go over to toddlers who do fall asleep quickly and pat their backs for a moment or snuggle them, since those children rarely get attention at naptime.

7 Have all children rest on their cots for a quiet time, even if they don't sleep. Most toddlers will take an afternoon nap.

8 Let children who wake up slowly make the transition by going to the bathroom and then playing quietly on their mat or at a table.

9 Enjoy the routine of naptime and avoid rushing through with the goal of getting all the toddlers to sleep quickly.

Moving Toddlers from Cribs and Cots

Programs handle the grouping of toddlers in their own ways. Some centers group children according to exact age, while other centers move children to a new classroom when they learn to walk or can stay on a mat during naptime. Many programs include the developmental needs of the child and the enrollment plan or availability of space in the next age group. All good programs teach parents and staff that the placement of a toddler in a particular classroom is not as important as the educators who create and ensure the routines, environment, and educational opportunities appropriate to each toddler. Each toddler should be comfortable and secure yet challenged to grow and learn.

So When Should Toddlers Move from a Crib to a Cot?

The move from cribs to cots should be made when children show signs of being able to stay on cots and not fall off. They should be ready to stay on cots and not roam during naptime. Lots of toddlers like to roam.

Crib and Cot Don'ts

Young children should view sleep and rest times as relaxed, comforting times of day. Cribs or cots should never be used as places where children are put for misbehavior. The use of sleep or rest as a kind of punishment teaches children that it is something unpleasant and should therefore be avoided or resisted.

Accommodating Parent Requests

Many people mistakenly believe that toddlers will sleep longer at night if they do not take naps during the day. If a parent requests that you awaken a toddler after three hours of sleep, it would be appropriate to turn on the lights in the room and let the child slowly rouse to the conversation and movement of the other children and adults. If a parent wants a toddler to skip an afternoon nap or sleep for only a short time, suggest that the parent speak to the child's pediatrician and provide you with a note indicating the benefit of this request for the toddler. Speak to your supervisor or director before approaching the parent.

Sleep is an important factor in toddlers' physical development, cognitive acuity, and emotional responsiveness. Although every child has different sleep patterns, most toddlers require daytime sleep. Making naptime enjoyable and productive is as important as meeting children's nutritional needs. Some children resist sleep and need your support and encouragement. The same is true for toilet learning. If you think naptime is hard, how about toileting? Let me ask you a personal question. Are you toilet trained? The majority of you mastered that task by the time you entered elementary school, and I think you'll agree that successful toileting is a life skill you can't live without. Ready to conquer potty training? That's next.

OPTIMIZE YOUR KNOWLEDGE

1 List two or three reasons why toddlers **need to nap**.

2 How can a toddler classroom accommodate **morning nappers**?

3 Create an appropriate **afternoon nap routine** for toddlers. Make a list of what would ideally happen.

6 Helping Toddlers and Twos with Toilet Learning

6

I am patient and encouraging when toddlers show signs of toilet readiness.

- Always
- Usually
- Sometimes
- Never

A Major Milestone for Toddlers

That first word, that first step, and, well, that first tinkle in the toilet are big deals in the lives of toddlers—for them and the adults in their lives. Whether you call it toilet training or potty training, you probably know that it's not really training at all. You can encourage and show toddlers all about the potty, but when they actually *go* depends on a number of factors, the greatest being the physical ability to *hold it*, for lack of a more technical term. You know what I mean.

Quick Caution: There's More to Toddler Life Than Toilet Learning

Although toilet learning is a major milestone and a big deal, the life of toddlers and their curriculum is more than just learning to go potty. It's hard not to let toilet learning become the dominant focus of the curriculum in a toddler room. Many parents and some teachers seem to view children who have mastered the skill as more advanced or intelligent, and that's not true. And there seems to be a great sense of accomplishment on the part of some toddler teachers when they can say about the toddlers in their classroom, "They're all trained!" No more diapers is a good feeling for everyone. Encourage toddlers, but remember that children learn according to their own readiness schedule.

When to Start Toilet Learning: 8 Signs of Readiness

The decision to begin the process of toilet learning should be made primarily by parents with the advice of teachers and, most importantly, signs of readiness from toddlers. Usually children between the ages of eighteen months and two years begin the process. So what are the signs of readiness?

1. The toddler can follow directions easily.
2. The toddler can pull clothing and underwear up and down.
3. The toddler's diaper is often dry for longer periods of time.
4. The toddler tells you that his diaper is wet or soiled.
5. The toddler knows when he is going in his diaper.
6. The toddler is interested in the bathroom.
7. The toddler wants to sit on the toilet or potty-chair.
8. The toddler is not experiencing any significant life changes, such as a new sibling or the death of a loved one.

What Do You Call It?

Even I am not going to list all the words for *pee-pee* and *poop*, although my ten-year-old son would love that. From what I've already written, you can see the language I tend to use. Asking a toddler, "Do you need to urinate?" or "Do you need to defecate?" seems a bit formal to me, but work with the parents to choose words their children understand and you feel comfortable with in your program. You have to call it something! I do believe, however, in educating children about their bodies and helping them to refer to their private parts by the correct names of *vagina* and *penis*.

Too Young to Start Toilet Learning?

My mother told me that I was potty trained by nine months. Sounds a bit young to me, and of all my four children, not one was out of diapers before two years, but every child is unique and every family is unique. Cultural expectations around toilet learning vary, as do parents' desires for toilet success. Economic reasons often drive parents' decision to have their toddler toilet trained. Diapers are expensive. Family expectations can often make parents want to start the process sooner rather than later, because the question, "He's not potty trained yet?" can leave them feeling guilty and inadequate. As I mentioned before, many people believe that sooner is better and that success indicates greater intelligence.

So what do you do when a parent asks, "Can you start toilet training my child?" It's your role to educate parents about child readiness and to help reassure them that a child's success in other areas is not dependent on mastering toileting. It's also acceptable for young toddlers to sit on the potty if they wish, keeping in mind that beginning too early often leads to frustration and power struggles between them and adults. There is no easy answer.

A Relaxed Approach Is Best

Somewhere between two and a half and three years old, the typical toddler learns to stay dry most of the day. Before this age, wide variation occurs in children's interests and abilities to toilet. A relaxed pace with a nonjudgmental approach is essential for toddlers' success. Remember: they are struggling for self-control, accompanied by all the complicated emotions of power, shame, failure, and accomplishment. Your job is to be calm and supportive, reducing the pressure that children feel. As toddlers show readiness, you can respond with help and encouragement.

If children are physically and emotionally ready and adults are not hyperfocused on toilet learning but take a more relaxed approach, learning will happen. The toilet-learning process is enhanced for toddlers who are in a group where they learn much from each other, including potty talk. They may develop an interest in sitting on the toilet when they see others doing so.

6 Toilet Learning Myths

MYTH # 1: Toddlers who are toilet trained at an earlier age are more successful in school and life. College applications don't ask, "At what age did you give up diapers?" Most children are ready to toilet learn between eighteen and thirty-six months. Even if they have mastered the potty at eighteen months, that's not an indication that they are headed down Ivy League Lane. And just because they haven't learned until three years old doesn't mean they're not going to Harvard. There's no direct correlation between success in school and life and the age they learn to go.

MYTH # 2: The smarter children are, the faster they'll potty train. Actually, bright, curious toddlers are sometimes so busy exploring the world around them that toilet learning is not a priority, and they may even resist toileting. A child once told me, "If you stop wearing diapers, you have to stop playing to go to the bathroom." Children are so smart! Toilet learning can take anywhere from a few weeks to a couple of months. So with the right encouragement from you, toddlers can learn at their own pace and take their time.

MYTH # 3: Good parents potty train their children by age two or earlier. Potty training isn't really training at all: it's potty learning. If you start potty training toddlers too early, they may be unable to physically do what you want. And teachers and parents may get frustrated because of accidents and children's lack of interest. Toddlers will go to the potty when they're ready, not when you, Grandma, the neighbor, or even the school is ready for them to go. Somehow, some way, almost all toddlers eventually train themselves, and that is the secret.

MYTH # 4: Toddlers shouldn't have many accidents during toilet learning. During toilet learning, accidents happen. And to you and the parents, it may often feel as if they happen and happen. Some children have lots of accidents and others only a few. Whether you use pull-ups, training pants, or underwear, have plenty on hand so toddlers can change easily after accidents. Having toddlers feel in control, even during accidents, is the best way to achieve success.

MYTH # 5: Children who are potty trained don't have any accidents. Even months after toddlers have successfully learned to go to the potty, accidents may occur. Remind them every hour while they are learning and continue reminding them until they are in full control. When toddlers are stressed about things that are happening—for example, a new home or worse, the divorce of parents, they may have more accidents. That's normal. When life smooths out, so will the accidents.

MYTH # 6: If adults really want to toilet train toddlers, they have to be tough. On the contrary—nurturing, positive, and patient teachers and parents foster learning success in any learning situation, and this is especially true with toilet learning. Try considering each accident *a near success* instead of a failure. Control your frustration when cleaning up accidents, and be positive.

The Home Connection

Toilet learning is often mastered in group care before it's mastered at home. This is because the routine and the we're-all-doing-this-together attitude is easier to maintain in child care than at home. So it's really important to communicate with families about your process and be supportive of their efforts at home. (Redleaf Press publishes a booklet for families about toilet learning called *Good Going! The Potty Training Guide for Families*, written by Gretchen Kinnell. It's a great resource to hand out to families.) If parents ask you what they need to know to get ready, here's somc information to share.

What Do Families Need to Get Started?

As with everything we do with babies and children today—feeding, sleeping, and toilet learning—there are lots of products to help make the process easier. Parents can decide what is right for themselves and their child. When they are ready to start toilet training, suggest they make a special date with their child to go shopping for underwear. The child can pick the type of underwear and then be treated to ice cream on this special potty day. The other thing to encourage families to consider is a potty-chair that sits on the floor. Children seem to have a greater sense of security with a small potty than with cold porcelain under, giant steps up, and flushing water below. We give children little spoons, little beds, little cups, and little books. Little potties just make sense.

How Should Families Encourage and Praise Their Children?

Nurturing, positive, and patient parents foster success in any learning situation, and this is especially true in toilet training. Reassure families that accidents happen. And often it feels as if they happen and happen. Some children have lots of accidents and others only a few.

Suggest that families create a toileting routine. Make potty time part of the everyday schedule, just like brushing teeth or getting ready for a nap. When they find that their child's diaper is dry after a nap, they can start the routine of heading to the potty as soon as the child wakes up. This will provide a better chance of success, because the child will probably need to go.

Dressing Toddlers for Success

Overalls and buttons on pants are often difficult for toddlers to master when they're rushing to the bathroom. Educate and encourage families to dress their toddlers in clothes that are easy to pull up or down. Elastic-waist pants work well for most toddlers. Sweatpants are also a great potty-learning choice. They absorb more of the mess during accidents and are easy to wash, and toddlers can get them off quickly.

Too Many Accidents?

If toddlers continually have accidents and rarely make it to the toilet, perhaps it's too early to start potty learning. The children are not really ready. With agreement from the parents, try switching back to diapers or pull-ups again. You can encourage the toddlers to tell you when they need a change. This way, they are letting you know they have gone, and that's one of the first steps in toilet learning. Toddlers must recognize that they have done it to learn to hold it.

Also, if toddlers seem frustrated, consider taking a break from toileting learning. It doesn't confuse them if you stop and start again when they are ready. In fact, doing so will lead to greater success for the children and the adults. Sometimes a break of a few months or perhaps just a few weeks can make the learning process happen almost effortlessly overnight.

Underwear, Training Pants, or Pull-Ups?

There are different views about pull-ups versus training pants versus underwear. It's really a parental preference. Pull-ups are definitely the easiest choice for cleanup; they are a bit expensive but great for trips in the car, places away from home, and naps and nighttime sleep. Training pants make cleanup a bit easier and save children's clothes from getting soiled, but they need washing. For many children who are ready to toilet, wearing underwear helps them experience the dribble-down-the-leg and squishy-in-your-pants feeling. These provide instant recognition that if they forget to go in the potty, it really feels yucky. They're often a greater incentive for young children to hurry to the potty than disposable pull-ups. The best choice depends on the children, their parents, and your guidance.

winning ways

Whether you call it **toilet teaching**, **potty training**, or **toilet training**, you'll agree that learning to go to the bathroom all by themselves is a huge milestone for toddlers. Make it a relaxed, fun learning and bonding experience for the toddlers and you. During the toddler years, children are learning to control their behavior as well as their body functions. They are learning about socially acceptable ways to interact and communicate their needs and wants. The next topic is about guiding toddlers' and twos' behavior in a positive and encouraging way.

OPTIMIZE YOUR KNOWLEDGE

1 List three signs that a toddler is ready to begin **toilet learning**.

1 ______________________________

2 ______________________________

3 ______________________________

2 Describe what you would **say and do** if a parent of a twelve-month-old child asks you to begin toileting learning.

____

____

____

____

3 Write what you would say to a toddler who has an **accident** and urinates in his pants.

____

____

____

____

7

Guiding Toddlers' and Twos' Behavior

7

I understand that discipline is not about punishment but about guiding toddlers to make safe choices and act in socially acceptable ways.

- Always
- Usually
- Sometimes
- Never

Misbehavior or Exploration?

When I am working with young children, I like to remind myself of how old the children really are. The toddlers you are working with are one or two years of age. Most of the clothes and shoes in my closet are older than that, and I may even have food in my fridge going on a year. How much could they have learned in a year, in two years? Quite a bit, as you may have experienced and this book outlines, but think about yourself and other adults. Aren't most people still trying to learn better self-control, how to express their feelings and needs, and how to act appropriately with others? Are your expectations of toddlers and their behavior really appropriate, or do you expect them to behave in ways they may not be capable of or that may require lots of practice to master?

Much of what gets toddlers into trouble actually occurs when they are doing their jobs in ways that sometimes drive us crazy or could result in harm to other people, things, or themselves. Remember the toddler's job description in chapter 1, "Toddlers and Twos Are Amazing"? Development is not free of mishaps and mistakes. Exploring a new world and testing new powers are not always easy. Try to think about these examples of seeming misbehavior more as exploration and learning.

- When toddlers push or bite, they are saying, "You are not my friend" or "You make me mad": the beginnings of socialization.

- When toddlers climb on the table, pull the dog's tail, jump on the bed, and scream as loud as they can, they are saying, "Look what I can do": the beginnings of self-expression and self-confidence.
- When toddlers drop a spoon, open the forbidden door, or put toys in the fish tank, they are saying, "What will happen if . . . ?": the beginnings of scientific discovery.

Are You Thinking That May Be a Stretch? Not Really.

Think of misbehavior as

1. A normal response to developmental growth
2. An opportunity to guide toddlers appropriately
3. An indication of ways you can work to eliminate problems and help children be successful

7 Ways to Set Up Toddlers for Success

1. **Toddlers need positive attention.** Some children require a great deal of attention, and that can be exhausting for you. It is often those attention-seeking children who may act up because they want even more attention. They may feel that negative attention is better than no attention at all. Try getting into the habit of rewarding the toddlers with your attention for positive behavior.
2. **Give toddlers some control by offering choices.** By giving toddlers some choices and a little control over their lives, you can often avoid resistance and inappropriate behavior.

   "Do you want to sit next to me or your friend?"

   "What color paper would you like?"

   "Where would you like to play first?"
3. **Redirect toddlers.** When children are upset or acting out, divert their attention by guiding them to stop or leave what they're doing and find interest in something else. You can use redirection in absolutely any situation or place.

   "Let's read a book while you are waiting for snacktime."

   "I know you want to play with that car, but Katie has it right now. Look at this car. It goes fast."

   "What do you think we can see if we look out the window? Let's go look."

4 **Have appropriate expectations.** Try to limit waiting time for young children. Arrange your routine so they don't have to be quiet or sit still for long periods of time.

5 **Have a routine that ensures toddlers are fed and rested.** Tired, hungry children are more likely to act out. Make time for rest during your day, if only for a few moments. Balance active times, like playing outdoors, with quiet times, like reading books.

6 **Decide what really matters.** When children want something, consider their requests carefully. Are they outrageous? Maybe they aren't. Be flexible and open-minded. Choose your battles; accommodate toddlers when you can.

7 **Acknowledge toddlers for self-control and efforts of self-control.** Some children have more difficulty than others controlling themselves. Praise toddlers when they use their words and/or regain control.

> "Thank you for asking me for more juice. Now I can help you. Good job!"
>
> "It's hard when you don't get to go first. You started to get mad, but you stopped and waited."
>
> "It doesn't feel good when you are out of control. I'm glad that you stopped kicking and could come back and join the story."

The Two "Oh, No" Behaviors of Toddlers

Of all the behaviors that toddlers exhibit, biting and temper tantrums are typically the ones that are the most challenging for you to deal with. These behaviors seem to cause chaos and uncertainty in the room while adults and other toddlers look on. Visceral responses run high, especially when it comes to biting. Parents and even teachers may want children who bite repeatedly to leave the program. Take a look at the sections below on understanding and responding to tantrums and biting.

What Is a Temper Tantrum?

A temper tantrum is an irrational, immature way of expressing anger or frustration. Throwing a tantrum usually involves exactly what it implies: toddlers throwing themselves on the floor, complete with kicking, screaming, and crying. While tantrums are inappropriate behavior, they are perfectly normal—and developmentally appropriate—for children aged one to three years. When you're with toddlers who are having tantrums, it's hard to remember that these outbursts generally diminish as children get older and develop better coping skills. Just about the time they move up to the next classroom, right? Yep, by three years, tantrums become less frequent because children learn other coping skills for dealing with anger and frustration. By school age, tantrums are rare.

What Causes Temper Tantrums?

Ever try to work some new sort of electronic gadget, only to find yourself tossing the manual, stomping your feet, and contemplating hurling the gizmo out the window? That's the adult version of a tantrum. Most of the time, toddlers who have tantrums are also struggling with frustration. Frustration in children may be caused by

- Hunger
- Exhaustion
- Inability to communicate that they want something or to do something
- Inability to produce a particular outcome—for example, work a toy
- Overstimulation; having too many things happen at once

Of these reasons that may contribute to a toddler's frustration, which situation is most likely to cause you to become frustrated? In other words, when are you most likely to flip out? Write the cause here:

____

Very young toddlers may be frustrated when you can't understand what they want, and older toddlers may get upset because they cannot put something together or get something to work. In these situations, the best response is encouragement and understanding. These may be enough to help toddlers avoid a tantrum.

9 Steps to Help Toddlers Who Are Having Tantrums

Some tantrums are brought on by children's frustration and fatigue, while outbursts may be due to attention-seeking or demanding behavior. Here are a few ways for you to support toddlers who are having tantrums:

1. **Try talking to the children if the tantrums are just beginning or are not too physical.** Validate the children's feelings:

   "It's hard to wait for food when you are hungry."

   "I know you wanted to be the first one to paint."

   "It's frustrating when you don't want to come inside."

   Help children to express themselves by offering assistance:

   "I understand you want to tell me something. Show me what you need."

   "I know it's hard to work this toy, but you'll get better at it. Can I help you?"

2. **Let the tantrum run its course.** Tantrums are either a means for letting off steam or a way for toddlers to try to get what they want. As long as children are safe, let the tantrum run its course.
3. **Avoid giving toddlers attention.** Do not give the children any attention, negative or positive. Giving attention to them may only reinforce the behavior as a means of obtaining their goal. As long as the children are safe, consider moving to another section of the room where you can still see them but they no longer have your direct attention.
4. **Do not try to reason with the children.** Temper tantrums are irrational responses to normal situations. Trying to reason with toddlers tends to make it worse.
5. **At the beginning or end of the tantrum, reassure the children.** Tantrums can be scary to children. Verbally encourage and reassure them:

   "I can see you are very angry. I'll leave you alone until you cool off."

   "I know you are very upset. I am here if you need me."

   In some cases, help the children regain control with physical contact. Toddlers who are having raging tantrums may not be able to regain control except by exhausting themselves. These children will be better able to regain control if you hold them. Try approaching them from the side and gently place your hands on their shoulders. Move your hands down their arms to help steady them. If they are on the floor, try sitting near their heads to avoid being kicked, and gently place your hand on their backs.

6 **When the tantrums stop, comfort the toddlers and offer alternatives to tantrum behavior.** After a temper tantrum, hold, hug, or let the children know in some way that you care about them:

> "You were really angry. Next time, use your words and tell me what you want."

> "I want to help you, but I can't do it when you kick and scream. Next time, point to what you need."

7 **Tell toddlers that having a tantrum is not okay.** Children need to understand that having a temper tantrum is never acceptable behavior:

> "It's not okay to act like that. [*Describe the behavior.*] You cannot lie on the floor and kick and scream."

8 **Do not give toddlers what they want as a result of the tantrum.** Giving in to the toddler's temper tantrums may momentarily cause them to stop the behavior, but it greatly reinforces their belief that acting in an inappropriate, angry way is the way to get what they want.

9 **Document children's tantrums if there are many.** Record the time and circumstances of each tantrum. Study the documentation to determine if there are times or situations in which toddlers are more likely to have an outburst. Use this information to anticipate and help them avoid a tantrum. If toddlers are more likely to have tantrums before their naps, schedule earlier naptimes.

With Special Care

A child over the age of three years who has frequent temper tantrums may have other issues precipitating this behavior, such as language and/or speech issues, medical problems, or stress related to home or school. Talk with your supervisor about meeting the child's parents to encourage them to seek help from professionals, like their pediatrician.

Every Bite Is Upsetting: How to Deal with Biting

As parents and teachers know, toddlers sometimes bite. And when they do, it's often hard for anyone to remember that biting is a common toddler behavior. It may be a few bites, and sometimes it's a lot. It may be one child who is biting or sometimes it can be a few children. The child who bites may focus on a single child or may bite indiscriminately. Regardless of the situation, every bite is upsetting, and every bite counts. Repeated biting is a pattern of learned behavior that is more difficult to extinguish because the child has learned that biting achieves results. Those results might include gaining a desired toy, drawing the attention of adults, even if it is negative attention, or creating excitement in the room.

Why Do Children Bite?

Children bite for a variety of reasons:

- Oral sensory exploration
- Crowding
- Seeking attention
- Intense desire for something
- Frustration
- Lack of language skills
- Learned behavior

What You Do When Toddlers Bite: 10 Tips

Although often no quick or easy solutions exist, here are some ways to try to extinguish the biting behavior:

1. **Avoid blame.** Biting is unfortunate but natural behavior. It is not something you can blame on children, parents, or staff.
2. **Be consistent.** Deal with each bite in the same manner.
3. **Document every bite.** Chart every biting occurrence, including attempted bites. Indicate time of day, circumstances, and others present.
4. **Look for patterns of biting.** Was there crowding? Too few toys? Too much waiting? Other frustrations?
5. **Analyze the patterns of biting.** Make any necessary changes in the environment, schedule, or routine to help the child who bites.

6 **Give positive reinforcement for not biting.** "I know you were really angry. Thank you for saying so!"

7 **Shadow children who bite.** Anticipate biting situations and teach nonbiting responses.

8 **Look at child groupings.** Analyze the grouping of children to avoid combinations that might lead to conflict or biting.

9 **Take every bite seriously.** Although biting can be normal and natural, treat each incident with concern and compassion.

10 **Remain calm.** Recognize your own frustrations and feelings when dealing with biting.

The Home Connection

It's important that parents understand that even in the best toddler programs, periodic outbreaks of biting may occur. It's best to have this conversation before a child is biting or has been bitten. Let families know that you have a plan to try to extinguish biting behavior. Here are some things to share:

1 When a child is bitten, we avoid any immediate response that reinforces the biting, including negative attention. The child who bites is immediately removed with no show of emotion. Caring attention is focused on the victim. The child who bit is not allowed to return to the same play and is talked to at an appropriate level and then redirected to another activity.

2 We look intensively at the context of each biting incident for patterns. Was there crowding, overstimulation, too few toys, too much waiting, other frustration? Is the child who bit getting enough attention, care, and appropriate positive reinforcement for not biting? Does the child who bit need help to engage in play or to make friends?

3 We work with each child who bites on resolving conflict or frustration appropriately.

4 We try to adapt the environment and work with families to reduce any stress on children.

5 We make special efforts to protect potential victims—for example, having teachers shadow the child who bit or the child who was bitten.

How Are You Responding?

"Do I Respond Appropriately to Unacceptable Toddler Behavior?"

Working with toddlers means you are going to spend the majority of your day guiding their behavior. How you respond to their actions and redirect them is critical to helping them gain self-control while maintaining self-respect. It's never about shame or guilt or punishment. Socialization is about helping toddlers learn to behave in a manner consistent with social values and norms.

Take a look at the following ten statements and accurately rate yourself on how you respond to toddlers' inappropriate behavior.

1 I stop what I am doing and go to the child.

Always Usually Sometimes Never

When you stop what you are doing and go to the child, you are acknowledging the inappropriate behavior when it happens and immediately correcting the child.

2 I speak to the child on eye level.

Always Usually Sometimes Never

For toddlers, this usually requires getting down on your knees, leaning over, or sitting on the floor. Eye level conveys your respect for children and your request for their attention.

3 I validate the child's feelings and express them in words.

Always Usually Sometimes Never

When children misbehave, let them know that you understand or that you are trying to understand how they feel. Validate their emotions or intentions. "I know you wanted the toy, but your friend was playing with it."

4 I speak in a normal but firm tone of voice.

Always Usually Sometimes Never

When you are redirecting toddlers or are upset with them, do not yell or raise your voice. Use a positive, natural tone of voice.

5 In simple terms, I explain to toddlers what they did wrong.

Always Usually Sometimes Never

Tell them what they did wrong. They may not know that taking books off the shelf is not okay or that a glass of milk close to the edge of the table may spill. Be descriptive with your words. Instead of saying, "You hurt Ethan," say, "You hurt Ethan when you hit him." Instead of saying, "You made a mess," say, "You took all the blocks off the shelf."

6 I offer children choices when possible.

Always Usually Sometimes Never

Whenever possible, give toddlers a choice. "It's time for nap. Do you want to put your blanket out by yourself, or do you want me to help you?"

7 I redirect children to a new activity.

Always Usually Sometimes Never

Guide children to a new activity and/or a new way of playing. "Please build with blocks. You can't play with blocks if you throw them. You can throw a ball. If you want to throw, let's go find a ball."

8 I tell children what the logical consequences for inappropriate behavior will be.

Always Usually Sometimes Never

Don't allow toddlers to continue doing what they want to do unless they do it appropriately. "If you keep writing on the wall, you cannot use the markers. Please write on the paper."

9 I follow through with what I tell the children.

Always Usually Sometimes Never

If you tell children that there will be a particular consequence for an inappropriate action, follow through. Remember to have appropriate consequences; see number 8. Consistency is very important.

10 I give toddlers positive attention.

Always Usually Sometimes Never

"You used the paint on the paper. Thank you! We'll hang it up on the bulletin board after it dries."

7 Final Tips on Guiding Toddlers' Behavior

1. **Expect toddlers to act like toddlers.** It's not a personal thing. Toddlers aren't out to get you. They're out to explore the world.
2. **Pick your battles.** Decide what matters a lot, a little, or not at all. Toddlers are learning so much during this period. Does it really matter if they have messy clothes or dump the toys out of the toy box?
3. **Redirect and avoid confrontation when possible.** Steer toddlers' attention to new activities or other interesting things by redirecting or distracting.

4 **Make life simple.** Prepare the environment and schedule to minimize frustration—for you and the toddlers.

5 **Anticipate frustrating situations.** Toddlers are more likely to be overwhelmed or to act out in crowded or unfamiliar places or when they are tired.

6 **Give lots of praise and encouragement.** Toddlers continually look for your approval and satisfaction.

7 **Enjoy toddlers for the wonderful, amazing people they are!** Toddlers become preschoolers almost overnight.

Toddlers often get a bad reputation with their full-of-life, I'll-try-anything mentality. Toddlers are bursting with energy and exploring their environment while trying to define themselves as separate people. They have an I-can-do-it-all-by-myself outlook on life but are easily frustrated when things don't go their way. Then they want you to do it. That desire for independence and need for your help (dependence) can be confusing and complex for toddlers and teachers. Since toddlers are focused primarily on themselves, sharing, taking turns, and waiting are all skills that will come in the later preschool years.

OPTIMIZE YOUR KNOWLEDGE

1 Name three characteristics of toddlers that can be difficult for you to deal with. After you have written your responses below, write the **positive attribute** of that behavior. I'll give you a couple of examples.

Characteristics of Toddler Behavior That May Be Difficult	The Positive Attribute of That Difficult Behavior
Hardly ever sit down	Learn with the whole body
Play in the sink	Explore with the senses

2 What would you say to toddlers to **validate their feelings** in the following situations?

▶ A toddler doesn't want to go inside because she is playing in the sandbox.

___

▶ A toddler pulls you by the pant leg over to a section of the room, but you don't understand what he wants.

___

▶ A toddler takes a toy from another child, and the toddler who had the toy first hits the second one. (There are two toddlers to validate in this example.)

___

___

3 Prepare a plan for a toddler who is repeatedly **biting** the same child. What would you do?

___

___

___

___

For All You Do

Of the three age groups discussed in this Winning Ways series, *Understanding Infants*, *Understanding Toddlers and Twos*, and *Understanding Preschoolers*, I think toddlers and twos are the greatest challenge. Why? Toddlers know so much more than they can do or express. They understand a great deal of language but can't yet speak well. They love to move but are still developing balance and can't always get their fingers to go the way they want them to. As it is often said, "Toddlers are long on will and short on skill."

Toddlers need teachers who are relaxed, patient, and responsive, teachers who enjoy the hum of emerging conversation and the busyness of almost constant motion. Is that you? Understanding toddlers will help you design a routine and environment to keep them safe to explore and learn. Understanding them helps you respond to the individual needs of all children and direct them in positive ways. Toddlers really are terrific!

Certificate of Achievement

This certificate is presented to

____

for completing the professional development program:

Winning Ways for Early Childhood Professionals: Understanding Toddlers and Twos

__________ In-service hours

Redleaf Press®
www.redleafpress.org
800-423-8309

Gigi Schweikert
www.gigischweikert.com

The author and Redleaf Press have not verified the actual completion of the program by this participant.